LifeNotes

Please note we have no control over the contents of other websites

Part of the *Compact Library* ™ published by

Compact Library Publishers ™

CLIP ™

Publishers Since 1953

all rights reserved to copyright, trademarks, and tradenames

Edited/authored by Paul Snyder – the editorial "we" is used to emphasize that most of the content was assembled by, and not original to, the author.

i

Contents

What is this?

It is a book about life, your life. It represents an objective, rational, search for a reason for living.

2

Who Am I?

The day you were born you began a learning process that will continue for the rest of your life. You were, from the beginning, molded by your surroundings, parents, relatives, playmates, by all the general attitudes, ideas, and beliefs you came in contact with. Each new year of life added to your past, changing the way you viewed every new day, influencing how you reacted to everything from the simplest daily routines to complex events touching you, your family, and the world you lived in.

As you grew older you interacted with people from different backgrounds with differing ideas about life. Faced with new ideas, you may have defended your beliefs, or you may have completely abandoned your past. However, like most people, you probably belong to that vast river of humanity which lives each moment in the easiest, most pleasant way possible. If so, you were and are more or less able to blend ideas, feelings, philosophies, desires, and realities to justify what you want to do.

Along with the majority of people, you were and are good at sending questions and ideas about the meaning of life and death, as well as thoughts and feelings about what is good and bad, deep into the cloudy regions of your mind. Whether we realize it or not, most of us are voluntary prisoners of our minds, unwilling to question who we are and what we believe, happy to simply roll along through life.

Most of us will live from birth to death in a world we have fashioned from our past to suit our present. Few will ever stand free from their present beliefs and daily lives to ask what is life about? Who am I? What should I do? What will I do? If there is meaning to life, and a reason for living, these questions must be answered.

If there is a true meaning to life, nothing that you do, say, or think will change that truth. What good is it to live your life believing what you are doing is right if your beliefs are false and what you are doing is wrong? It is an understanding of life that we seek, a search for something in life worth living for.

Recognizing what you find requires you to open your mind and accept whatever you discover, even if it is totally opposite to your experiences, beliefs, and wishes. Your willingness to understand is a willingness to grasp the very reason for your living. If the answers you find are different from those you have molded for yourself, you must decide whether to continue on the path you are on or go another way on a new path toward a new destination.

If You Are Who You Are, Then Who Are You?

Each of us is born, we live lives of various lengths, and then we die. We have a separate nature which is our own and which sets us apart from every other person who lives or has ever lived. We share similar characteristics, but each of us is unique. You are you.

What makes us unique is the fact that we perpetually make choices between alternatives. Our choices seem to be far more than mechanical selections based on some complex biological decision making scheme. Rather, your choice seems to be based not only on what you believe will happen if you make a certain choice, but also on what you "want" to happen. You engage in what we will call "rational thought", whereby you think about many things, including the concepts of right and wrong. You eventually reach a point where that certain quality of being which is unique to you takes over, and you make your choices.

Even though human beings have instinctive feelings for self-preservation, self-satisfaction, etc., you can choose to do the opposite, to go against what your instincts, personality, and emotions tell you to do. You can think about what you are going to do and can choose to do what you believe is right and good even if it places you in grave danger. Similarly, you can choose to do what you believe is wrong and evil even if you would instinctively do otherwise. Your decision is your decision, a product of your singular existence and being. Able to engage in rational thought, and to choose freely among various courses of action based on those thoughts, you are in a very real sense what you choose to be.

Who Will You Be When You No Longer Are?

Warning! There is a risk that as you read our book you may think that we are suggesting that there is no "reason to live". That is not what we are saying at all! In fact we are saying the opposite, we have abundant hope that you will find in yourself the reason for living. If you are discouraged or depressed, please finish reading all of this book. Anyone who is, or becomes, seriously depressed should always seek immediate medical help. See Distress & Depression at the end of our notes.

If in fact you do exercise meaningful freedom of choice, what good is it to be a unique human being if at your death you cease to exist? If you do not continue to exist in some form after death, what good are all the experiences, decisions, triumphs, defeats, all the moments of your life? If you do not survive the grave, if you return to the state of being that preceded your birth, then we suggest to you that nothing in fact does matter. While over the ages men and women have sought to perpetuate themselves through their children, their place in history, their role in society, and through intricate philosophical webs of existentialism and other essays on physical human beings' importance, the fact of physical death remains. If each generation's death means the end of those individuals, then we are all faced with an endless cycle of creation and destruction, the meaning of which, if any, is beyond comprehension.

If there is anything in life we can count on occurring without fail it is physical death. The successful bank president, the champion athlete, the homemaker, the famous, the unknown, every human being, you, die. While all acknowledge the certainty of their eventual demise, few think about death until they are faced with it. The simple fact of death is not news to anyone, yet the reality of its impending occurrence is ignored by virtually every living person.

The very nature of human life denies death and shrouds it in the cloak of future events, events that are not yet real and do not need to be dealt with in the present. Living is too important and time consuming to be concerned with mortality. The fact that you are moving steadily toward your death is most likely, and literally, to be the last thing on your mind.

Observing the inevitable death of every creature that inhabits the earth, we may have a recurrent feeling that death is the end. On the other hand, it is virtually inconceivable to us that all we are, all we have been, all we will be, may be rendered void in that moment of death. It goes against human nature to visualize the effective destruction of our past, present, and future, which may accompany death without existence beyond death. Yet if each human being does cease to exist, then all human beings are, or in the case of generations yet unborn will be, waiting their turn to cease existing. If each and every human being ceases to be, then the feeling of continuity that pervades the human race may be false (please note, we do not believe that life is in fact destroyed by physical death).

In their arguments for humanism, existentialism, etc., philosophers have spent lifetimes trying to construct a difference between the apparent continuity of humankind, and the periodic death of individual humans. Most of us think of our ancestors as a link to the past, and our children as a link to the future, yet if we do not survive the grave each generation may die an isolated death that mocks any assertion that humankind has a continuing existence apart from its individual members. If each person's death results in their no longer existing, then no manner of historical recording, social progression, or other remembrance in the minds of those whose time to die is yet to come, can in any way affect, preserve, or make any difference whatsoever to those who no longer are. No one will survive to remember. If each of us ceases to be, then your life may have no meaning and your choices may make no difference.

We admit that this logic seems counter intuitive, and even wrong, but if we are willing to dissociate ourselves from the incredible biologic urge for self-preservation, both of the individual and the species, and are willing to apply purely objective reasoning, the logical conclusions, while discomforting, are perhaps inevitable (there are several possible logical loopholes that might give permanent meaning and value to a finite physical life, we discuss them in more detail in our other books). This is a very difficult conclusion to accept, it goes against our intuitive feelings about human life, and against our assumptions that individual physical lives have meaning and value.

Yet if we are little more than doomed animals, our intuitive feeling of meaning and value would not be surprising. From the very beginning, to assure survival of any species, evolution would certainly have instilled in living creatures the feeling that there is a reason for them to exist, a reason for them to crawl out of the ocean and build cities. If there is no life after death, and our lives are in fact consumed by "nothing", it is no wonder that our genetic heritage argues so strongly against that possibility.

Think about it. If each person's consciousness is the product of their physical brain, then it seems logical to assume that individual physical consciousness exists only during that person's physical life on earth. If each of our physical lives proceeds from birth to death, then the consequence of each person's death necessarily follows their death. Who can be affected by that death? Certainly those who survive may be affected, but here is the "problem", the death cannot be of any consequence to the purely physical human being who no longer exists. The moment before the death of a human being it can be said that their impending death affects them, but the very moment after the person dies, he or she is no longer around to be affected!

Most agree that cause and effect, action and consequence, occur in a fixed order, the former always "preceding" the latter. Let us assume, for example, that a comet hits the Earth and all life is annihilated. It is very hard to accept, but if consciousness, our mind, is nothing more than a physical phenomenon, if there is no non-physical continuation of life after death, then the most logical conclusion is that the complete annihilation of humankind is of absolutely no consequence to humankind!

While the words may sound bizarre and counter intuitive, in fact they may not be. The moment after the total destruction of humankind there is no humankind left to be affected. Indeed, there is no humankind around that is conscious of the fact that the comet struck the Earth!

The same logic applies to the history of individuals not visited by a catastrophic event (note that our logic may be questioned by those who think we live in a timeless block universe, we believe it is valid in all physical models of our universe). If you believe that each human

9

being is nothing more than an individual physical entity, and therefore that there is no life after death, then at the time of their death each human being experiences the identical individual annihilation that all humankind would experience together if the earth was destroyed by a comet.

If a human being named Bill dies at 12:00 noon, and there is no life after death, at 12:01 Bill is not "around" to be affected by his death. After 12:00 noon you could search the entire universe for Bill and you would not find him. If there is no life after death, the very moment after the event known as Bill's death, Bill no longer exists, and Bill cannot be affected by anything, including his death.

The logic goes even further. If you do not believe that human consciousness continues to exist after physical death, then death not only annihilates each individual's present and future, but also annihilates their past. Most people would agree that for an object to have a present and a future the object must exist. Many would make the distinction that while an object cannot have a present and a future if it does not exist, it somehow can have a past. It is clear that the present and future of an object are bound to the existence of the object, but so too is the object's past.

Much of the problem lies in the use of the words past, present, and future both to describe that which is part of an object (a "past" which belongs to the object, like a person's memories that "belong" to the living individual from birth to death), and to describe the existence of the object from a third party's view (a "past" which is a chronological description of an object, like a photo album containing a lifetime collection of pictures of an individual who has died). It is a misconception to equate the fact that there is a "history" of all beings or objects which is set in the "past", with the statement that a being or object that no longer exists has a "past". The first idea simply says that the being or object existed over a finite period that is apparent to those who currently exist. The second idea is different, there is a "history" set in the past that is the sum of all lifetimes, but a person who no longer exists has no "past" that is their past, unique to and dependent on their existence. A person who has died has no physical past, present, or future for the simple reason that the person no longer exists.

Admittedly, our conclusions about physical death are totally opposite to our "common sense" understanding of life. There are many arguments that purport to counter our logic, including assertions that a person's life before physical death has "existential" meaning (we use "existential" in the sense of having meaning and purpose "in and of itself"). Yet most, perhaps all, of the relevant alternative arguments are based on the biophysics of existence before physical death. They are set in the time before death, within the causal sequence of events that precede death. We believe that none of the arguments adequately address the period after physical death, and therefore none answer the question of how a person who no longer exists can be conscious of, and be said to possess, a past, a present, or a future.

You Can't Think About Nothing

Even though we are convinced that physical death is not the end of your existence, if it is the end should you be frightened by the certainty of your demise? If indeed you cease to exist, you need not fear death, for after your death you will feel neither pain, nor pleasure, nor peace, nor torment. "You" will no longer exist, therefore "you" will feel nothing. The resulting void is just that, a complete and total void.

There would be nothing to fear, for there will be no one to experience anything negative. There would be nothing to look forward to, for there will be no one to experience anything positive. The only way you can visualize what is usually called a "nihilistic" death is to picture yourself after death as being in the same state you were in before birth (of course you were not really in any state at all). Such a fate would leave nothing to be feared.

Philosophers often speak of the void that would follow physical death without life after death as the abyss, the unknown, the approaching void, etc. All of these suggest that we are on a journey to a "place" which lies at the end of our physical lifetimes. If on our death we cease to exist, this idea that we are traveling to our ultimate destiny is false. We are not traveling to an abyss, the void, or the unknown, for these words suggest that we are moving toward something. We recognize the seeming absurdity of the language, yet if on our death we cease to exist, then "nothing" totally consumes us.

This is the heart of the problem, we cannot in any way whatsoever understand or visualize "nothing". When we think about "nothing", we turn it into "something" that can be thought about. The moment we attempt to comprehend or visualize "nothing", we interject something into "nothing", preventing us from reaching our goal. The only way we can answer the question "what is nothing?" is to answer it by not asking it, for if we ask the question we destroy the answer. If we are no more than physical beings, and if "nothing" follows our physical death, then at the moment of our physical death, "nothing".

The possibility of "nothing" absolutely frees us from any concern we may have about a physical life that has an end, and demands that we

13

live for the possibility, however slight we may believe it to be, that there is "something". We discuss why this is true in the next chapter.

Afraid of Nothing?

What should our response be to all of this? We strongly believe that there is absolutely no reason not to live for the possibility that life has meaning and value. We think we are right about the transitory nature of physical consciousness, but we may be totally wrong. If we are wrong, if each of us has a singular physical consciousness that somehow survives physical death, or if there is some other form of existential existence that gives meaning and purpose to our physical lives, then our life may have meaning and value even if there is no non-physical life after death. We will not pursue this possibility, yet you should recognize that it might, or might not, exist.

A brief comment on the word possible. Saying something may be possible is misleading in the case of mutually exclusive options. When we say there is a possibility that our conclusions are wrong, or a possibility that there is no non-physical life after death, or a possibility that there is existential meaning without a non-physical life after death, we are talking about facts that are either true or false. Our conclusions are right, or they are wrong, either there is a non-physical life after death or there is no non-physical life after death, either there is existential meaning absent a non-physical afterlife or there is not. If life has no meaning without a non-physical existence after physical death, and there is no life after physical death, then there is no "possibility" of existential meaning. If there is existential meaning to life without non-physical existence after death, then the possibility of existential meaning exists and always has existed.

If in fact there is no non-physical life after death, then there is no possibility of a non-physical life after death and such a possibility never existed. Yet if there is a non-physical life after death then the possibility, indeed the actuality, of life after death exists and always has existed. Whenever you see the word possible, and similar words like might or may, remember that if something does not and cannot exist, then that something is and was never possible (the probability is zero). If something can exist, then that something represents an actual possibility.

15

If we are right, if our consciousness and existential physical being do not survive physical death, our death may mark the end of our existence. Yet if our physical consciousness dies, it is still quite possible that we will not face a "nihilistic" death. Perhaps we have a non-physical consciousness that survives physical death, and that gives meaning and value to our lives.

Beyond the human desire for meaning in life, we would suggest that the logical consequences of what philosophers call a nihilistic death require the search for alternatives to nihilism. Those who believe that the nihilistic void is approaching are, by the very nature of their humanity, required to search for something to believe in other than the void. While it appears to be impossible to scientifically prove that life has meaning and value, it is equally impossible to prove that life has no meaning and value. No matter what the person who concludes that life is meaningless believes to be true now or at any other particular time in their life, the possibility always exists that he or she may eventually find true meaning and value.

The following is very hard to explain and may take several readings and a great deal of effort to understand. The limits of human comprehension make it extremely difficult to recognize the fact that if there is a nihilistic void after physical death, then there is absolutely no reason at all to think about the "nothing" that may follow physical life. Nothing cannot affect our physical lives, either positively or negatively. It cannot be a part of our existence, it cannot be a part of our thoughts, it is "nothing".

If after our physical death there is "nothing" then when we die we will not experience calm or peace or pain or distress, we will not experience anything because we will not exist. "Nothing" will not relieve us of anything simply because there will be no one to experience relief, there will be no "you" who can feel the absence of pain. You will not remember the good times or the horrific events in your life. We need to accept the difficult but essential point, if nothing follows physical death then there is no peaceful sleep because no one exists who can sleep, there are no nightmares because there is no one to dream. All will be as if it never was.

If you live five years in excruciating pain and there is nothing after physical death, then when you die the pain does not "end", it is as if those five years never happened. If you live fifty years in excruciating pain and there is nothing after physical death, then when you die the pain does not "end", it is as if those fifty years never happened. If there is nothing after physical death, you gain nothing if your physical pain lasts only five instead of fifty years, there is no difference. In both cases on the day of your death the excruciating pain does not "end", it is as if the pain never was.

There is a profound difference between pain which ends and pain which never was. It may seem that anything which results in pain being as if it never happened is an end to the pain we are suffering, but that is not a true description of the "reality" of not existing, of "nothing". Take the time to really think about the difference, you will eventually realize that if on our physical death our past is consumed by nothing, it is no worse to suffer fifty years of pain than suffer five years. If in fact there is nothing after physical death, then if you live one minute, or 20 or 30 or 40 or 50 more years, all the horrors in your past, present, and future will be "consumed" by nothing. This is not the same as saying that we find "peace" in a nihilistic death, we find "nothing". All will be as if it never was.

Similarly, if you live a long and comfortable life filled with personal accomplishments, and there is nothing after physical death, then on your physical death "nothing". If there is nothing after physical death you will have no past. It will be as if you were never born, as if you never existed. All will be as if it never was.

If there is nothing after physical death, there can be absolutely no benefit to a shorter life, no logical reason to want physical life to end. Even though it may seem absurd, if we do not exist after our physical death we have no reason to fear, or avoid, five years or fifty years of the most horrible pain.

The all-consuming nature of the "nothing" that may follow physical death is what human beings find almost impossible to comprehend. Yet understanding the possibility of "something", life after physical death or existential meaning to physical life, and the freedom of "nothing" if we are wrong, allows us to live as long and as good a physical life as possible.

If you are living a pleasant life your initial response to the possibility of "nothing" may be that it is frightening, or if you are suffering it may feel somehow comforting, both thoughts are totally, unquestionably, wrong. If on our physical death there is nothing, then there is no rational or logical reason to think about physical death as fearful or

17

peaceful. If there is nothing after physical death then the experience of physical death (perhaps it is better to say the experience that never happens) is the same if it occurs in one day or one year or one hundred years, during a period of great joy or great pain. There would be "nothing" in your future to look forward to, there would be "nothing" in your future to fear.

If you really understand what this means, you recognize that the possibility of nothing allows us to endure all the physical and emotional pain we experience no matter how horrific, and to live the most positive life we can with the hope that there is a non-physical life after our death. It is very important to recognize that nihilism can never lead to suicide, for nihilism tells us that if we do in fact live in a nihilistic world, nothing that happens in our lives, no matter how painful it is and how badly we may feel about it at the time, has any "real" consequence at all.

If there is nothing after death, then it makes no difference to you if your life was filled with pain or pleasure, because you will not exist to feel pain or pleasure. Yet if there is an existence after death, then by having chosen to endure physical pain and chosen to live the most positive physical life you can, you may find after your physical death that memories of even the worst pain are overwhelmed by "joy" and "disappear". If there is an existence after physical death, then enduring a lifetime of physical and emotional pain may result in a timeless eternity of peace and happiness.

The possibility of nothing leaves you absolutely free to live a life filled with both pain and joy, knowing that if you live in a meaningless world the pain will be as if it never was. Terminating life never brings release from pain, rather it may destroy the possibility of a meaningful, perhaps joyful, non-physical life. If there is an existence after death, and you choose suicide, you may be rejecting that peace and happiness. We are absolutely convinced that the philosophical neutrality that nihilism demands, means that nihilism never suggests or in any way supports suicide as an option for any human being.

If you believe that suicide is an option, you totally misunderstand what you have read, you do not comprehend what it means to say that "nothing" may consume your past, present, and future. You do not understand what it means to say that all will be as if it never was. You need to reread this book until you understand that nihilism renders false all arguments for suicide.

Again, if you find yourself distressed or depressed by our conclusions please read Appendix B – Distress & Depression.

Is That All There Is?

If it is true that your existence ends with physical death, does that mean that your life is meaningless? As we have said, our answer is probably (but not certainly) yes. Therefore, is it true that your life has no meaning? The answer is no. If we are somehow more than our physical bodies, if we can exist beyond and apart from those bodies, then perhaps each of us survives physical death and continues to exist, in some manner and form, beyond the grave. If you are, or you become through living, a unique individual who possesses the ability to engage in rational thought and exercise freedom of choice, perhaps you have an existence beyond your physical mind and body.

Since the dawn of recorded history people have thought and written about existence beyond physical death. Some have suggested that extra sensory perception, premonitions, unexplained knowledge of past events, etc., are part of the world beyond death. Perhaps the unique being which each of us is, the present existence that makes your choices and your life yours alone, exists now and after your death in a realm beyond the physical. Perhaps each of us continues to exist in a manner and fashion infinitely beyond our ability to imagine, let alone comprehend, perhaps not.

A great number of people have spent vast amounts of time and effort studying all manner of phenomena outside everyday experiences. Many, most, or even all "inexplicable" events may be explained by future generations of scientists. We have little difficulty accepting that there are events which are in fact controlled by forces beyond our present knowledge. If they are true phenomena, and not products of the mind, their very existence strongly suggests that there is a world which is quite real lying somewhere beyond normal human perception.

There are no present answers to the questions posed by what many perceive to be "metaphysical" events. Our book deals with what the meaning and purpose of life is. As we continue you will see that the question of whether or not anyone has witnessed supernatural phenomena originating from a world beyond the grave is not important. You will see that even if no one ever has any contact in this world with a world beyond the grave, it does not mean that such a world does not exist. We simply don't need to look for metaphysical events in our lives to understand what life is all about. At this point we ask that you keep an open mind about life after death. For now, please accept the possibility, however remote you may feel it is, that in some manner and fashion we continue to exist after our physical death.

The Search for Truth

If a scientist, philosopher, or anyone else tells you something is true, and in fact it is not true, it is not true. To say something is true does not make it true. Even though you are told something is true, if it is not true it is simply not true. On the other hand, if something is true it is true, even if you are told or believe that it is not.

Science is based on observation, formulation of theories, and more observation. To observe necessarily requires the ability to perceive, to sense, feel, smell, touch, taste, see, hear. Early humans used all their senses to explore the world around them. When human senses proved inadequate, they devised better and better tools and instruments to extend their range. Microscopes and telescopes to expand vision, stethoscopes and amplifiers to increase hearing, along with thousands of other devices.

The catalog of devices used to expand our human senses is enormous and growing by the minute, yet all the instruments of humankind can do no more than extend the reach of humans into the universe of which they and their instruments are a part. We know of three spatial dimensions, height, width, depth, and a fourth dimension, time. Physicists suggest that there are many more unseen dimensions. How many dimensions are there? No one knows, for there may be any number of dimensions which are separate and beyond human ability to sense, measure, and thus scientifically prove.

Does that mean that additional dimensions do not exist, the answer is no. If a dimension exists, it exists. If a dimension does not exist, it does not exist. This is true regardless of whether we can, or never can, observe that dimension. No matter how many dimensions are eventually observed, one or more additional dimensions may or may not exist beyond human ability to observe.

Many of you are saying to yourselves, it is one thing to say that a dimension beyond human ability to observe may exist but an entirely different thing to say that one probably does. You are right. Most of you will go on to say it is highly improbable, maybe less than one chance in a trillion, that even one more dimension exists beyond the observable number of dimensions, however many that may eventually prove to be. If you think that, you are wrong.

To be able to statistically predict the likelihood of an event happening we must first observe to see how often the event occurs during a given period of time. If we cannot observe the event when it occurs, we cannot determine how often it happens (or does not happen) and we cannot calculate the likelihood of the event (mathematical models may predict the existence of that which cannot be observed, but they cannot contribute to statistical proof).

The problem with recognizing the limitations of statistical analysis and science is understanding the difference between not observing an event where the event watched for can be observed, and not observing an event where the event cannot be observed because it is beyond human ability to sense. The first, not observing an event which could be seen, leads to the valid conclusion that the event is unlikely to occur. The second, not observing an event which is beyond human ability to perceive, beyond experimental observation, cannot lead to any conclusion at all about the reality of that event. Yet it appears to be human nature to assume that things which have never been observed do not exist, or at best are highly unlikely to exist.

If something exists beyond human perception it will never be observed during our physical lifetimes. If you cannot measure something because it is beyond human perception you cannot prove it exists, on the other hand you cannot prove that it does not exist. More importantly, you cannot say that it is likely or unlikely that it exists! You simply cannot say anything objective at all about that which is beyond human ability to observe.

It is very, very important to realize that it is absolutely impossible to say that it is either likely or unlikely something exists beyond human observation. We simply cannot determine in any way the probability that something exists, or does not exist, beyond our observable universe. To understand the significance of this often overlooked statement is to understand that we have absolutely no idea what, if anything, lies beyond our human boundaries.

Because we cannot know what lies beyond our perception or how it might affect our physical reality, we can never prove that anything is absolutely "true", or absolutely "false". A moment's thought should bring the realization that this absolute limit of statistics and science renders all "scientific proof", as well as subjective feelings, that nothing exists beyond our perception into "philosophic arguments".

Despite what science might claim to have "proven", and despite what we might "feel", about what lies beyond our ability to observe, we cannot say anything objective about that which is beyond human perception. No one, not you nor I nor the smartest person on earth can say that it is likely, or not likely, that a "world" or "worlds" exist beyond the physical world in which we live. From an objective standpoint anything, or nothing, may exist beyond human cognition.

The Mystery of Existence

Entropy is a measure of disorder. If you pour cream into your coffee, the cream will never remove itself to make the coffee black again. This is because the entropy (disorder) of the system (the coffee with cream) tends to increase over time. As a rule, systems tend to become more disordered.

The universe we live in is a place of amazingly low entropy, if that was not true we would not be alive. Every star, planet, rock, tree, living creature, every human being, everything in the universe that is more ordered than the diffuse interstellar gas clouds that surround us, is an example of a system with low entropy. For our universe to have the extremely low entropy it has required at the "starting point" the selection of a single low entropy universe from a virtually infinite number of possible high entropy universes.

Sir Roger Penrose, a noted British mathematician who along with Stephen Hawking established how singularities form in black holes, concludes that: "There is a certain sense in which I would say the universe has a purpose. It's not there just somehow by chance. Some people take the view that the universe is simply there and it runs along, and we happen by accident to find ourselves in this thing. I don't think that's a very fruitful or helpful way of looking at the universe, I think that there is something much deeper about it, about its existence, which we have very little inkling of at the moment."

To be more exact, in his book "The Emperor's New Mind", Penrose calculated that the universe we live in required the selection of one out of 10 raised to the 10th power raised to the 123rd power of all possible universes! This is a deceptively large number, which in fact cannot be written. If you tried to write it out by writing the number "1" on a piece of paper, you would have to write a 0 on every single atom in the universe just to approach the number of zeros that follow the one, even then you would not be close to writing out the entire number" (see www.ws5.com/Penrose).

If this interpretation of modern cosmology is as solid as it seems, it means that the chance that our universe was created at random is as close to impossible as we can get! Note that the popular argument that the odds are more favorable for spontaneous creation of living organisms is not relevant. Creation of the low entropy universe in which life could evolve is fundamentally different to spontaneous creation of life in that universe. It is the odds against the random creation of our universe that approach infinity, not the probabilities of spontaneous creation of life in our universe.

Many find comfort in believing that even if science has not yet discovered what they are, every physical event from creation onward evolved according to a set of absolute physical laws. The mathematically precise physical structure of the universe, the tiny place we have in the incredible vastness of space, the biologic characteristics we share with animals, etc., all may be interpreted as evidence of a purely mechanistic process that governs our lives.

Yet if we consider the complexity of that which we observe, the initial extraordinarily low entropy of our universe, matter which should not have survived antimatter, the mystery of consciousness, and if we are honest with ourselves, we cannot escape the intuitive feeling that there is an "order" in the chaos which cannot be explained by science. Even if the odds against the random selection of our low entropy universe out of all possible universes are not quite as impossible as they seem, we simply cannot ignore the intuitive feeling that the odds are almost infinitely against the spontaneous creation and existence of everything around us.

No matter how strongly we may feel that life is the result of physical processes only, if we are objective we should conclude that it intuitively seems impossible that a random physical process could create the almost infinitely complex, yet extremely well ordered, low entropy, universe in which we live. Anyone who takes the time to try to visualize billions of stars bursting out of a pinhead faces a mystery which, at the very least, leaves us with the possibility, however slight, that the observable physical universe is not "all there is".

Even if science eventually finds an answer to what appears to be an unanswerable question, "how" was the physical universe created, the ultimate question "why" does the universe exist will remain. "Just because it does", as well as other anthropomorphic explanations, seem less than satisfying answers. What all this tells us is that we have no real objective idea at all what the true nature of our life is, or what the possibilities are for our continued existence after death.

28

Love

The love we are talking about is far more, incredibly more, than that which we normally call love. Love is the most positive of human experiences. It is the deepest, most profound, of human relationships. It is the giving of all you have to give to someone else.

What is love? Love is beyond definition, it cannot be described in words. No effort to describe love can in any way answer what love is. Love is beyond human ability to analyze and evaluate.

Yet each of us has, as a part of our very being, an understanding of love. The love we are talking about is basic, profound, a fundamental part of our existence. In each and every one of our hearts and minds, and we believe souls, we know and understand what love is.

Love is so deeply a part of human beings, so far beyond definition and description, so elusive to those who halfheartedly seek it, that you will know and understand love only if you engage in a very personal search of heart and mind and soul which leads to the very essence of your being. To understand life it is necessary to understand love. No one can make you understand love, you alone must be willing to take the inward journey. We will repeatedly urge you to do so, for nothing can take the place of that understanding.

Most of us think we already know what love is, when in fact few do. Sometime during our lives the majority of us will believe we have found true love, even though we have not. Many of us will go to our graves believing we have loved when we never loved at all.

For most people, their understanding of love is hidden deep within. Each time they glimpse love and feel it trying to surface, they push it back to its resting place. Few are willing to search for the love that may be found inside them, few are willing to let their knowledge of love surface. We believe each and every person who truly wants to know and understand love, and who is willing to search and search and search their heart, mind, and soul, will know and understand love.

Truth, Belief, & Faith

We have discussed the fact that we can never be certain anything is true. We have considered the limitations on human understanding which make all human assertions of fact simply statements of belief. Does all this mean that what we believe to be true but cannot prove is any less true? Again, the answer is no. If something is true it is true whether or not you prove, believe in, or have even thought about, its truth.

Literally billions of ideas and beliefs can be suggested to be true. We can propose assumptions which will send us off in any direction we might wish to go. We can argue that we are descendants of Martians, that inanimate objects talk to each other, etc., etc., etc. Every day we see people who are certain of the absolute truth of their beliefs, never realizing they have talked themselves into accepting as absolutely true that which is, and must be, based on their assumptions.

Since we cannot know whether or not something or someone exists beyond our perception, we cannot know if the wildest of ideas may in fact be true somewhere outside our current existence. Yet even though "anything" may be true, we should not allow ourselves to apply logical arguments to first "prove", and then "disprove", fundamental beliefs about the nature and meaning of life. What we want is for you to put aside your assumptions and beliefs; take a journey into your heart, mind, and soul; and then decide what you want to believe is true.

What is true is true. What then is the difference in believing something to be true, and proving something is true, if indeed the belief is true? The difference is not in the truth of the matter, for the belief itself is either true or not regardless of any belief as to its truth. Rather the difference lies in the realization that what appears absolutely true may or may not be true.

If we cannot prove anything, how do we determine what is true? If the best we can do is believe something is true, what good is that? The

29

answer lies in what we just said, if what we believe to be true is true, then proof is not necessary for that truth.

We have been talking as though we start with the belief that everything we seek to prove is untrue, and then go from there. The fact is that we have built into our existence a set of assumptions that certain things are true, assumptions we base our strongest beliefs on. For example, though nothing can be proven beyond doubt, few would argue the world they live in does not actually exist, or a ball thrown into the air will not fall back to earth, or people do not grow older. Few doubt or question the solid reality of any of the events that make up everyday life, from the proposition the sun will rise to the reality of everyday tasks associated with living.

All you are, all you have been, everything about your life contributes to your belief in the truth of millions upon millions of things. Your life, and your perception of it, is an incredibly intricate web of observations, feelings, and experiences, all parts of your existence, all making you, you. Perhaps humans have some inexplicable intuition that gives them insight into what is actually true, perhaps not. The fact is that all anyone can do is to use all the abilities they have to determine what is true. All you can do is think, and analyze, and test, and rethink, until you believe something is true.

In many cases the scientific method serves us well when we search for the "truth". This is particularly so when we sort through results of objective tests to analyze which drug is most effective, what car is best, etc. In other cases logic proves inadequate and "feelings" seem to be a better guide.

Philosophy and religion are not suited to scientific inquiry. Because they deal with that which is beyond human perception, philosophical and religious beliefs must come from within each individual and must be based on all that makes an individual a unique human being. Such beliefs grow when experiences of life combine with that illusive quality that makes each of us the singular person we are.

How much, if any, of the process of determining fundamental beliefs is guided by insight, and how much is a product of heredity and environment, is a question without answer. We have seen many people paralyzed by the fear that what they believed to be true might be false. Over the years we have come to believe that if anyone puts a sincere effort into determining what is true, and what is good, they will succeed. Even though they will never be able to "prove" anything, what they find themselves believing to be true and good will be, perhaps even if not perfectly correct, what actually is true and good. There is, of course, no proof for such a belief, yet for us it is fundamentally true.

We are not suggesting that someone who has determined his or her answer to a question before searching for it will ever find the true answer. Those who want to prove their point, even if it is only to themselves, will inevitably mold everything to fit their answer. With varying degrees of discomfort, they will reach their previous conclusion every time.

What we are saying is that we are convinced that those who search their hearts, minds, and souls to understand life will find themselves believing certain things to be true and right. Perhaps these more or less inherent beliefs are simply products of human existence and thought. Perhaps, however, they are insights into profound fundamental truths.

What about the times when you feel strongly that something is or might be true, but are uncertain of those feelings because, to some degree, your beliefs lie outside human perception or experience? Beyond mere "belief" is something called "faith". When our beliefs are strong we may choose to have faith in their truth.

What then is "faith"? In part faith is having an intense conviction what you believe to be true is in fact true, but it is more than that. Real faith in the truth of something is a product of your total being. It is not only what you believe to be true, but what you want to be true. Faith is a total commitment by you to believe that what you think should be true is true, that what you think should be right and good is in fact right and good.

You cannot have faith in something or someone simply because there is nothing better to believe in. Faith cannot be based on negative choices, but must be based on a real, strong, sometimes total, desire that what you believe should be true actually is true. You must want what you have faith in to be true. Since nothing can be fully proved or disproved unless truth has been somehow revealed, that which people have faith in is, for them, that which is true.

What is worth having faith in? Earlier we said if your existence ends with the death of your body it is virtually inconceivable to us that life has any meaning at all. We believe that your existence has meaning only if you continue to exist in some form or fashion after the death of your body.

The End May Be Just the Beginning

Just because we cannot prove something is true does not in any way mean it is not true. Because we cannot prove, or disprove, we continue to exist after the death of our bodies does not mean that we do not continue to exist, or that we do. If we continue to exist after our physical death, then we continue to exist, and if we do not, then we do not.

We believe that if there is to be any reason and purpose to your life you must prove or believe or have faith in an existence beyond the grave. Since it looks like no one can prove they continue to exist after death, the question is whether or not you choose to believe you do. Yet existence beyond the grave lies so far beyond human perception and observation, beyond human comprehension and understanding, that human feelings about such existence are inadequate to base fundamental beliefs on.

Then is this a matter you should have faith in? Your answer to that question, if it is to be more than a casual one which will not last, must be based on what you believe life is "all about", not only after death but also right now. If you are to have faith in a life after death you need to believe people are more than biologic creatures. To be worth having faith in, to be worth wanting, life beyond the grave must be more than just existing through time. It must offer a hope of something worth living for, of "goodness", perhaps of joy.

We can imagine many different things about life beyond the grave. We may believe in a metaphysical extension of life, somehow self-perpetuating and dependent only on a communion of some sort of mental energy unique to human beings. We may believe in reincarnation, whereby forms change but human beings never die. There is no limit to what we may believe life after death will be like. As we have said, no one can prove us wrong, or right.

Speculation about the "physical" nature of life after death can be nothing more than guesses and offers little help in making a decision whether or not we would want to live in such a world. If we are more than our physical selves it would seem that there must be more to look forward to in a life after death than the "physical" aspects of that life.

We need to find out if there is something beyond the physical that every human can have faith in if they want to be more than worthless travelers in time.

If we survive the grave, does it not seem intuitively likely that the most positive aspects of our life on earth will also be positive features of the world after death? In looking for a reason to believe in an extension of life beyond the grave that is worth living for, and thus worth having faith in, you must look at this world and this life. Life on earth is the only basis we have on which to project what a world beyond the grave might be like. You must find the most positive aspects of this life, you must find in this life a reason to believe life has meaning and purpose.

Perhaps you will find "good" in this world that gives you a reason to believe, or have faith, there is a life after death filled with "joy". To help you choose what to believe about life, now and beyond the grave, we need to explore our present lives. In the rest of these notes, we will be considering whether there is "good" in this life that makes it worth having faith in a life after death.

If we do continue to exist after our physical deaths, then each moment of our lives, both before and after death, may have meaning and purpose. If we survive death then each of us has been, is, and will continue to be a unique being. What then is the meaning and purpose of life? What should, or must, you do? What choices do you have right now?

Many philosophers, psychiatrists, and others, argue persuasively that self-satisfaction is the most important human goal. A society made up of individuals who maximize their own wellbeing is a society at its best. They conclude that when each of us reaches our own point of maximum pleasure, all of us benefit.

What constitutes the maximization of pleasure is a hotly debated question, answered in countless, totally different ways. Ideas range from doing anything that makes you feel "good", to espousing intense dedication to such diverse things as political causes, meditation, or simply the pursuit of pleasure.

Many suggest the free market works well in selecting what is worthwhile in life, with various methods of providing pleasure coming and going as demand identifies, supplies, and satisfies needs. Others argue the best society is made up of family groups that seek to maximize the family's happiness. Some extend the group to include friends and even strangers, but often exclude those outside the group's geographic and social spheres. Volume after volume after volume has been written describing what various people believe life is all about. Multitudes of people have dedicated large parts of their lives to convincing others of the truth of their ideas and the wisdom of following their examples.

Instead of closely examining and eliminating one at a time what we believe to be the fallacies and follies of humankind, we will suggest to you what many believe life is all about. If you choose to know and understand what is said, we believe you will discover what is true and gives meaning and purpose to life. We are about to look for something in life worth living for, something to have faith in. What many suggest is worth living for is love. Not what we often call love, but that which is the most profound of human experiences.

The search is difficult, it is perhaps the most difficult task you will ever face. If you search your heart, mind, and soul you will find yourself surrounded by multitudes of conflicting feelings, questions, doubts, etc. These will draw your attention away from your search and may make it seem futile and worthless. If you try to deal with each distraction as it appears, you will end up floundering from side to side, without direction, your goal appearing on the horizon yet never getting closer.

Before answering the many questions love poses, before satisfying your doubts, you should complete your search. Search your heart, mind, and soul, your being, to know and understand love. Set aside all questions, doubts, and fears, put all your energy and thought into your search. First understand love, then ask and answer questions about it.

It is very hard to stay on track. Your search will take you through and among daily experiences and deep memories filled with the emptiness, cruelty, and physical pleasures of a world where love is seldom seen. The cold glance of strangers on the street, the reality of poverty in the shadow of enormous wealth, watching people get sick and die a seemingly final death.

Thoughts of food, drink, luxury, sex, all the physical pleasures you could be enjoying. All these pull at your attention and cause your mind to drift. Your focus is blurred as first one thing and then another interrupts your search.

Even when you think you have broken through the fog and are running toward your goal, a tiny diversion, a moment's pause, and you are flung back into that strange and cloudy state of doubts, not knowing where, if anywhere, you are. Back in the haze, you may find yourself believing you reached your goal when you did not. This feeling of success can be strong, and the rush of living may make it seem even more real since little time is available to stop and think about who you are, where you have been, and where you are going. What can happen is that you can make yourself believe you understand love, when in fact all you have seen is false illusions of love. You may wrongly conclude that love is really not that special at all.

To allow yourself to stop short of your goal, to allow yourself to believe you understand love when you do not, is to condemn yourself to the deep darkness shared by all who live without love. A darkness few recognize, a blackness the depth of which can be appreciated only by those who find love. Only those who finish their search will know and understand love.

Completing the search requires a willingness to start. It is far easier to live your life following whatever sort of daily routine you have over the years consciously and subconsciously constructed for yourself, a routine designed to make you feel good about your life. For most of us this means mixing with our daily activities that bring us self- satisfaction and physical pleasure, just enough "good" deeds to give us the illusory feeling that we are "good" people. For better or worse you nurture an image of yourself you have been developing since childhood. An image that dictates what is expected of you and rules how you act, making your life a repeating cycle of yesterdays.

Even if you do not feel good about your life, you are usually more comfortable not straying too far from the familiar. It is easier to live the life you have made for yourself than it is to question and search and change. Yet if you want to know and understand love you must give the search your all, without fear of, or resistance to, the changes it may bring in your life. You need to search and search until you know what it means to love, what it would be like to live in a world where each and every person loves every other person.

This is more than a mental exercise. If after your search you believe love is what all people should give each other, then you have perhaps not only found what gives life meaning and purpose right now, but also found that which makes it worth having faith in life beyond the grave. At this point we are not suggesting that you embrace without question the ideas of eternity and the goodness of love. We are saying you will find it virtually, or perhaps totally, impossible to decide whether or not to believe that love is worth living for, if you do not know and understand what love is. Only when you are willing to search your heart, mind, soul, your very being, to know love, will you understand the decision to love or not to love. Only then can you make your choice.

In the remaining pages we will give some examples of love, discuss what those who love do, and talk in general about love. Yet nothing we say will bring you an understanding of love, only your search can do that. Your search will begin whenever you want it to and will end whenever you want it to. This book is useful only if you take the hours, days, months, or years, whatever it takes, to complete your search. If you stop when you find that half-hearted, fleeting, shallow thing most people call "love", your efforts will have been futile and worthless. You will have failed to find what love really is.

It is very easy to stop short of understanding love. The idea of pure, real love is so alien to our experiences, so foreign to the world we live in, we subconsciously, and even consciously, reject it as a non-existent fantasy. Yet it does exist. Because we seldom, if ever, witness such love does not mean it is less than real. Because the experiences of our past and the realities of our daily existence attack love does not mean it is a fantasy. We may never choose to fill our world with pure love. Yet because each of us can choose love, such a world is possible. Our doubts and fears, desires and temptations, weaknesses, and longing to "live", cannot change the fact that pure, true, real, love exists, and that people can love one another.

What Do Those Who Love Do?

If you love someone who is hungry, you will give them food; someone who is thirsty, you will give them water; someone who is cold, you will give them your coat. If you love someone who is sick, you will care for them until they are well; someone who is in prison, you will visit them; someone without a home, you will take them home with you. These are all acts and deeds those who love do for the people they love. Yet love is far more than the doing of any particular act or deed.

While those who love people will do the things we just mentioned, simply doing "good deeds" is not the same as loving. Many who do not love do "good deeds". Many who say they love, and perhaps even believe they love, if they love at all, do so only halfheartedly and from moment to moment.

It is hard to say that someone who feeds a person when they are hungry and then leaves them to find their own shelter really loves that person. It is hard to call love the giving of money to an orphanage when children's cries for attention and companionship go unanswered. It is difficult to understand how someone can say they love a person when they make that person feel they need to applaud their donor for every gift they receive.

Love is far more than acts, deeds, words, or feelings. To love someone, really love someone, is to give them all you have to give, true, deep, pure, indefinable, indescribable love. It is giving to others the love that you will find and understand if you complete your search of heart, mind, and soul. What we are talking about is love, true, pure, real, love.

If you love, you will help a stranger who needs help, even if it puts you in danger. If you love, you will think first about the needs of those you love, and only then think about your own needs. If you love, you will do what you can, all you can, for everyone you meet. Those who really understand love know in their heart, mind, and soul that love is the greatest thing in life one human being can give another. If you truly love someone you are giving them your very best.

We have reached an awkward point in trying to use language to describe a state of being which affects the totality of human existence. How can we adequately describe how a person who truly loves thinks, feels, and acts? We can't. So how can you understand what we are saying when we say love is the greatest thing one human being can give another.

Unless you have completed your search of your heart, mind, and soul and know and understand love, you will not understand what anyone is saying when they tell you about the love they find in their heart, mind, and soul. When you complete your search and know and understand love, you will know and understand that love is indeed the most positive element of human existence. You will know that the very best each of us can do is to love. Once you understand love you join all others who have completed their search in a communion of knowledge which makes communication of ideas about love easy and makes what is said clear.

At this point you should sit back and think about what is being said, for in these few pages we have jumped from looking for something worth living for, to the suggestion that you search yourself for an understanding of love, to the idea that all people should love one another. If you have not searched your heart, mind, soul, your very being, and do not yet understand love, what we are saying may seem interesting but not profound.

We wish we could think of words and logical arguments that would make true, pure, real, love, crystal clear to you, but we can't. We are simply not talking about the kind of understanding that comes from reasoned analysis. We could fill these pages with elegant prose and poetry describing love, yet not one word would have the power or effect that even a fleeting inward glimpse of love has.

Your Best Is Good Enough

The following will be very difficult to read and accept if you have not completed your search of your heart, mind, and soul. As you read please do not reject what is said. Complete your search, know and understand true, pure, real, love, before you make your choices. Take all the time you need, days, weeks, months, years, to search your heart, mind, and soul to know and understand love. Search your very being, until you know and understand what it means to love everyone with true, pure, real, love.

If you understand love you know loving does not require you to mechanically follow a set pattern of "right" actions. You know instead that if you love you will do the best you can in every situation, even if you cannot determine what the real solution is. If you love you do your best, and doing your best is something you can always do. Doing your best simply requires that which you are capable of, nothing more.

This does not mean loving is any easier because you do not have to know what the "correct" answer is. On the contrary, to say love requires you to do your best is to say that love requires of you all you have to give. Love requires everything you can give, your total effort. By requiring only that which you are capable of giving, it is always your choice whether you love or don't love. If you understand love you know it is your choice and your choice alone, to love or not to love. It is a profound responsibility to be able, every moment of your life, to love or not to love.

If you love another human being you are giving that human being your very best. If you love every human being you are doing the very best you can do for each of them. Similarly, if they love you they are doing the very best they can for you. It is not hard to see that a world where each and every person loves each and every other person would be the best possible world.

Since each of us can love if and when we want to love, a world filled with love is very much a possibility. Pure love is so rare a quantity in daily life it may seem almost impossible that, if they are willing, people can love all other people. Yet they can. We can bring about a world filled with love, a world that is worth living for.

Few seriously expect to see a day on earth when all people love one another. There are too many people for whom physical pleasure is more desirable than love. Only the most optimistic hold hope for a world filled with love. So, what is the next best world?

If you understand love you know you can love people even if they do not love you. You can always choose to love, and if love is the best you can do, does it not seem true that you should love even if you are not loved? Does it not seem true that you should always choose love?

If life ends with physical death, perhaps the proper response to hate would not be love but would be some form of resistance to hate that minimizes its influence on others. Yet that cannot be true if our conclusions are correct. We have already explained why we believe that if existence ends with physical death the "nothing" that would follow death would cause any response to be as if it never was. What if life continues after death, would it matter what we do when faced with hate?

If life exists beyond the grave, and if love is the best part of life in this world, does it not seem intuitively likely that if life after death is to be good it will be an existence filled with love? Of course we are dealing with questions beyond human ability to answer, we are in fact in the murky area where intellect, insight, and intuition blend with belief and faith. There is no way at all we can say anything concrete about what life after death may or may not be like. Yet there exists a "feeling" that at least a portion of whatever lies beyond the grave, if anything, possesses the positive characteristics of life in this world. If we come to believe the most positive aspect of life is love, then it somehow seems intuitively true that if those who choose to love on earth enter a life after death, it will be a life that is filled with love.

So, what is our answer? Who should you love? If loving is good, the question really becomes is there anyone you should not love? If you understand love you know you can always love someone even if the person you love hates you. When you hate those who hate you, you are doing the same wrong to them they are doing to you. The natural reaction is to hate those who hate you, yet if you understand love you should, after deep thought and consideration, reach the conclusion that since you never have to hate, you should always love (in our other

44

books we discuss if we should love someone who has totally rejected love).

What if the person who hates you continues to hate you, and does all kinds of evil to you and to others without sign of remorse? Again, if you understand love you know you can always love another person even if that person hates you. If we agree that the best we can do in this life, and in a life after death if one exists, is to love each other, the answer seems clear. If it is your choice to love or not, you should choose to love every moment of your earthly life. That means you should love even if you are not loved, even if you are hated.

If love is worth living for in this life, it is worth living for in whatever life may follow death. If it is possible that we continue to exist after death, it would seem that we should love now with the hope that when we die we will pass into a life where love will not only continue, but will be shared by all who join us there.

What should I do?

Loving someone does not mean you should support the wrongs they do. Many people who love others and try to help them out of problems like gambling, drinking, casual sex, etc., find themselves defending the other person and slipping into their way of life. There is a fine line between being with people and loving and helping them, and in an attempt to reach them accepting at least part of their way of life. If at all times you keep in your heart, mind, and soul what it means to truly love, you will have no trouble knowing where that line is.

If you choose to love, you will constantly have to decide what you should do in particular situations. The natural tendency is to take a middle of the road position that seems to be positive toward everyone involved without being too negative toward yourself. You then declare that your decision is based on love, and all seems well. Loving is not that easy, every single decision about love must be made from your heart, mind, and soul.

If you want to love you must search your very being for the answers love requires, and you must be willing to accept without change the answers you find. You are driving home from work, heading for a birthday party your spouse and friends have been planning for you. Traffic is heavy on the highway. You see a man hitchhiking, he seems unsure of his footing, as you get closer you can tell he is drunk. If you stop you are sure to be late for your party, anyway, there are lots of cars one of which is bound to pick him up, and he doesn't look like he will stagger into the roadway.

You think, "he may be pretending to be drunk so he can rob somebody, a policeman is bound to drive by, I can call one on my mobile phone". Time to decide what to do. You want to drive on by him and not have to decide, but you know you have to stop or not stop. You stop your car, help the man into the passenger seat, he mumbles the town he is going to and then passes out. You try to call your spouse but get the answering machine. When you reach the right exit, you get off and try to rouse your passenger. He gets sick and throws up, you stop to let him get some air and to clean out the car.

You're forty minutes late for your party, and your spouse is still not answering. You think about leaving him at a gas station, but you help him back in the car and go on. He sees a bar, yells for you to stop, and curses you when you don't. You arrive in his hometown, but he is too drunk to remember where he lives. You find a motel, get the hitchhiker a room, and pay the desk clerk to look in on him to see he is all right and to bring him breakfast the next morning. You buy him some clean clothes and put them in the room.

You call home, your spouse answers and then slams the phone down. Finally you arrive home three hours late, your guests have gone, your spouse and kids are mad, you are hungry and cold. You think about all the hassle you went through; the party you missed, your party; the drunk hitchhiker cursing you. You think, I hope I never get into another situation like this one, but if I do, I'll do it all over again. If you have not completed your search you may not understand the love given the hitchhiker. If you have, you know that if you choose love you would do the same things the driver did.

If you love someone, whether they are your child or a stranger, you will do the very best you can for them. If you love someone you will do the best you can, every moment of your life, even if it means that you do not have enough to meet your own needs. You will have compassion for every human being who does not have enough to eat, and you will invite them to eat with you.

You will care for those who are sick until they get well. If you meet someone who is homeless, you will find shelter for them. You will spend time with those who are lonely, and you will listen to their problems. You will help them not because it makes you feel good, but because you love them. You will give them the love that is in your heart, mind, and soul.

If when you look at someone you are looking for something in them that makes you feel good, whether that may be sexual attractiveness or delightful conversation or something else, you are not giving them the love that is in your heart, mind, and soul. If you love someone, when you look at them you do not have thoughts about their physical appearance. If you love someone, you do not think about what their personality is like. If you love someone, you do not think about whether or not you want to be around them and be their friend. If you love someone, you do not have thoughts about whether or not they make you "feel good". If you love someone, when you look at them you have love for them in your heart, mind, and soul.

If you give someone true, pure, real, love, you will love them, and you will not think of them as someone you do or do not want to be around. You will love all people, including those who other people consider to be ugly or dull or stupid or inferior. When you look at them you will not see someone who is ugly or dull or stupid or inferior, or anything else, you will see someone you love. When you look at them you will not see someone who is sexually attractive or vivacious or funny or popular, you will see someone you love. If you give to everyone the true, pure, real, love that is in your heart, mind, and soul, they will be more than your friends, they will be your family who you love.

Sit back and think and think and think about loving people with true, pure, real, love. Take all the time you need to feel and experience the love inside you that you can give to all people. Complete your search of your heart, mind, and soul and know and understand love.

You choose love, that means everything is all right, right? In a very real sense the answer to that question is yes, for you everything is all right. Everything being all right does not, however, mean that your life on earth will be physically better. It will probably get much worse, for those who choose not to love will be doubly hard on those who do.

If you love someone you will not hit them when they strike you. You will give them food, and drink, and shelter even if they hate you and even if you end up not having enough for yourself. If you love them you will help them when they are sick, even if they have cheated you and cursed your stupidity. You will love them no matter what they do to you, with the knowledge that you are doing what all human beings can and should do.

What if the choice comes whether to kill someone, or be killed by them? We cannot see how someone could choose to intentionally kill someone they love. Let us simply say it seems to us that if you continue to exist after death, and if it is true that if you love someone you will never kill them, then you have nothing to fear if because you love you die and enter an existence filled with love.

You never "have" to commit any violent act against another, it is always your choice to do so or not. If love requires rejection of all violence against another human being, those who understand love should understand it is worth enduring pain in this life if accepting such pain leads to love, both now and in whatever existence follows death. Death followed by a joyful eternal life of love, day after day, year after year, millions of years after millions of years, forever and ever and ever and ever, seems far superior to a pleasant life followed by a loveless eternity. We need to remember that no matter how hard we try to avoid our inevitable deaths, the fact is that we live lives that are no more than single grains among the infinite sands of time (additional comments can be found in the Appendix A – a Fanatic Life or a Normal Life? and in our other books).

If love is right, even one decision not to love is wrong. When you complete your search perhaps you may not agree with us that you will never inflict physical harm on someone you love. The answer you find to this question, and other questions less dramatic but as hard or harder to answer, is to be found in your knowledge and understanding of love. After you have completed your search, and know and understand love, you will have to decide for yourself whether or not our answer to the question about killing, as well as our answers to the many other difficult questions, are based on love, or not. We believe they are, but perhaps they are not.

We believe that after you complete your search of heart, mind, and soul you will know and understand that if anything is true, it is true that every moment of their lives each and every human being can and should love each and every other human being. Indeed, if every person chose to love every other person as they would have those people love them, if every person chose to love every other person as himself or herself, then each of us would do the very best that we could do for every human being in the world. There would be nothing more that we should do for each other, nothing more that we could do.

One essential warning, when faced with a hard question the normal human response is toward self-interest, with elaborate arguments to justify the answer and make it seem to be the result of love. The answer dictated by love is often (for some people almost always) very, very, hard to accept. Yet we are convinced that if you choose love you will accept the toughest of answers, and will find peace and hope in your decisions. At all times you must be absolutely certain that your answers are based on the knowledge and understanding of love you find in your heart, mind, and soul. You must be certain that you always choose true, pure, real, love.

Each moment of hate is a moment when you could have chosen love. If love is best, what could possibly be better than choosing to love every moment of your earthly life?

Forgiveness

We have said you can choose to love any time you want to. This is true no matter what you have done in the past, and only requires that you want to love now. If you decide to love, what can you do about your past?

The only thing that can be done is that you can be forgiven for having not loved. If you understand love, you know that if you love someone you will forgive them the wrongs they have done to you. Think carefully about love and forgiveness, and you will understand that if you love someone you will always and repeatedly and truly forgive them for having not loved you.

The murderer who admits his wrong and seeks forgiveness is perhaps better off than the cheat who denies he has done anything wrong and rejects any thoughts about needing forgiveness. If we have all done wrong, and if those who love forgive, should we not quit trying to keep score of each person's wrongs and forgive them? If you love people, you will forgive them. No matter how many times they may ask you to forgive them, if they seek your forgiveness and you love them, you will forgive them.

What about those people who don't want forgiveness? If you have completed your search and know and understand love, you know and understand that if someone is your enemy and hates you, you can and should love them. If you love people who hate you and do not want forgiveness, you will love them and do good to them with the hope that they will choose to love you and seek forgiveness.

If you love someone you will forgive them for everything they do to you and to other people. You can and should love both those who love you and seek forgiveness, and those who hate you and do not seek forgiveness. To love those who hate you and who laugh at your forgiveness is perhaps the greatest test of your desire to love.

Forever

If you understand love you know that if anything in life is worth living for, it is for people to love, really and truly love, people. Yet if death is the end, what use is it to love anyone? We believe that if death is indeed the end of your existence, then love and hate and you and I and life are all transient puffs of smoke in an ultimately inanimate eternity. Even love will succumb to death, making its apparent beauty no more lasting than a winter's snow.

We really do not know, and will not know, what lies in store for us beyond the grave until the inevitable moment of death arrives. If life and love end at the grave we will never know the answer for we will no longer exist, and the question will die with us. Of course, as we explained in the chapter Afraid of Nothing, such an end would be painless, all will be as if it never was.

We said that the possibility of "nothing" frees us to live the most positive life we can. There is absolutely no reason not to live for the possibility that life has meaning and purpose, and for the possibility that we may eventually find true meaning and value in our life.

We said there is absolutely no way we can prove life continues beyond the grave, we also said there is absolutely no way we can prove it does not. While we cannot be certain that life does not have meaning and purpose even if there is no life after death, we reached the conclusion that life has meaning only if there is a non-physical life after death.

If love is worth living for, and if the only realistic alternative is nihilistic death, then it seems that you, and I, and everyone else, should love each other and live for the possibility that we will continue to exist after death in an existence filled with love. Yet choosing love because the alternative may be a meaningless death is not a good enough reason. Love must be chosen by those who in their heart, mind, and soul truly want to love, or their choice will be a shallow one that will not last. Those who choose to love must do so because they want to love.

If we want to love, we believe that for our love to have meaning we must have faith that we continue to exist after our physical death. Can we have faith in a random existence after death that has no guidance, might there be more? If we are to accept that human beings may continue to exist after the death of their bodies we need to consider what, if any, external force or presence may "guide" or "control" such existence. We are way past the limits of human comprehension, at the point where belief must turn into faith. The more modern science has discovered, the more it seems that some form of "logical", rational, process occurs in nature, replacing random events with planned sequences.

Such logical progression of nature may be the result of an incredible computer like property whereby nature is equipped with some sort of "artificial intelligence", perhaps so, perhaps not. Yet we have already said that the odds that the universe was created at random appear to be as close to zero as can possibly be imagined. Perhaps the universe is not controlled or guided by some deterministic process. Perhaps the universe is controlled or guided by someone. [Please read the next section in its entirety before reaching your conclusions.]

God

Throughout human history there has existed in the majority of people a belief in some power, existence, a logical presence beyond human existence, a God (or gods). During at least the past few thousand years there has appeared in many cultures a belief in a God who is good, a God who wants human beings to do that which is good. Those who have completed their search of their heart, mind, and soul, know and understand love. Those who have completed their search know and understand in their heart, mind, and soul that it is good for people to love each other. Many believe that a God exists who gave us the love that is in our heart, mind, and souls. Many believe that a God exists who wants people to do that which is good, to love each other.

This belief in a God who wants people to love each other has its roots in intuitive feelings of humankind and in messages of prophets; and for those who believe in the divinity of Jesus, in the word of God himself. There will always be arguments that the messages are messages made up by the messengers, yet from all that we have discussed, from all that those who have completed their search know and understand about love, it seems that if God does exist the message from him would be for us to love one another, what many tell us it is.

We believe there is in most of us a feeling that God does exist. That feeling may be insight, or it may be the result of a collective deep seeded desperation in human beings to be more than doomed animals. We will not know until our death, the definitive answer forever prohibited us by the limits imposed by our being no more than a part of that which we seek to explore. We are left at the point where faith must take over if we are to believe in the existence of God.

Perhaps the "logical" selections that appear to take place in nature cannot be explained by physical processes, but rather represent actions taken by some indescribable presence, God, perhaps not. If our intuitive feelings and the scientific calculations that support them are correct, then the complex low entropy universe in which we live cannot be the result of random chance. If we are honest with ourselves, the only reasonable answer we can construct from objective observations based on current scientific knowledge as to why the low entropy universe in which we live exists, is that it was designed and created to be as it is. If a Creator does not exist then the logical conclusion is that the universe in which we live would not exist, and we would not be here.

Some people who believe that God does not exist, believe that human beings can love and do good in a purely physical universe where there is no God. Is it possible that they are right? If human beings want to do good, can they really do that which is good and meaningful if God does not exist?

If there is existential meaning to physical life that we do not or cannot understand, then perhaps even if God does not exist, love may have meaning. We can never be certain that life does not have existential meaning. We cannot prove that if God does not exist and there is no life after death then living our lives, and doing that which is good, has no meaning. Because of the limitations of being only human, we simply cannot rule out any possibility.

We said that, even though we cannot prove anything and may in fact be wrong, we believe that if we do not have a non-physical consciousness that continues to exist after physical death, then those who believe in nihilism are correct, and some type of "nihilistic" void awaits all of us. It may be a true void, like the void that preceded our birth, or it may be a very strange void where billions of copies of us merely co-exist in a relativistic block universe (we discuss this in our other books). Whatever physical form it might take, it would seem to be a "meaningless" void. All would be as if it never was.

If physical death does annihilate our physical past, present, and future, then our life has meaning and purpose and value only if after our physical death our consciousness continues to exist in a non-physical life. We cannot prove that we continue, or do not continue, to exist after our physical death. Yet if there is a life after death, then it is reasonable to conclude that you will continue to experience a non-physical existence after your physical death, and that your life does in fact have meaning and value.

Is it possible that even if God does not exist, there may be a non-physical existence after death which gives meaning and value to our life? The intuitive answer seems to be no. We cannot imagine a human spirit that survives death if there is no presence beyond life other than human spirits, if there is no Spirit greater than the human soul. It seems intuitively unlikely that the only non-physical presence in the universe could be the human soul.

If there is no non-physical Spirit greater than the human soul, if there is no God, it makes no sense to conclude that a physical being born into our physical world has at birth, or somehow develops, a non-physical soul. We can see no possible way that a physical human being, who is a tiny part of an unimaginably huge universe, can survive physical death if there is no Spirit, no God, to grant that "physical being", in some manner and fashion beyond our understanding, a non-physical soul and life.

It somehow seems intuitively true that without God there would be no reason to believe that we possess a "consciousness" that continues to exist beyond the death of our bodies, no reason to have hope that after our death we may live forever in a non-physical world. Even though it cannot be proven, it seems intuitively clear that if there is no Spirit greater than the human spirit, if God does not exist, then then there is no human soul, and we do in fact cease to exist on our death.

Should we believe that God exists? If we were presented with the question of believing or not believing in the existence of a god of war or destruction, then it would not matter to us if he existed or not because his existence would give us no hope that love has meaning and is good. There would be no hope for an existence after our physical death in a heaven filled with love. We would choose not to believe in the existence of such a god.

However, the message of many about God, the message we accept, was and is that God wants every human being to do that which is good. The message that we choose to believe is true is that if God exists God wants every human being to love every other human being. We choose to have absolute faith that if God exists, God is good.

Saying that if God exists, God is good, does not "prove" that God exists, it does not even say that God exists. It says that if God exists, God is good, period. It says that if God exists, God is good, and that he wants each and every person to do that which is good. Even if you do not believe that God exists, or you are not sure what the "good" is that God would have us do in this world, in your heart, mind, and soul you know and understand that if God, the Creator of love, exists, God is good.

If you do not want evil to have power over good, if you do not want evil to fill the world instead of good, we cannot imagine why you would not choose to have absolute faith that if the presence greater than all else in this universe, the Supreme Being, God, exists, God is good. Whether you believe that God exists or that God does not exist, if you do not want to reject good and embrace evil, if you are not against good and for evil, there is no reason not to have absolute faith that if in fact God does exist, God is good.

It seems intuitively clear that if God, the One who is good, does not exist then there is no "heaven" where there is a life after death that is good. It is intuitively impossible for us to imagine the existence of a good life after death in a heaven filled with love where there is no Spirit greater than the human soul, where a God who is good is not present. We cannot imagine a heaven filled with perfect love that is "created" or "sustained" by imperfect human souls, who during their physical lives repeatedly fail to choose love.

We cannot imagine a heaven filled with real, true, pure, love without the presence in heaven of One who loves with perfect love, without the presence of One who is good. It would seem that only God, the One who is good, could forgive human sins and "cleanse" human souls so that heaven would be filled with love. Without the presence of God who loves with perfect love, we cannot envision a heaven where human beings share real, true, pure, love. We cannot "prove" anything to be true, yet it seems intuitively clear that if God does not exist, there is no heaven.

We simply do not believe that there is a life after death in a heaven filled with love if God, the One who is good, the One who loves with perfect love, does not exist. We may be wrong, life may have existential meaning, yet it seems intuitively, rationally, logically true to us that without God each of us ceases to exist on the day of our death, annihilating our past, present, and future. It seems true that without God, good and love and life are empty ideas that live and die with each human being.

We may "believe" that God exists, yet rather than belief, is the existence of God something we should have "faith in"? As we have said, having faith something is true is far more than believing it is true. We can say that those who have faith accept as true what they choose to believe is true, at least until proven beyond doubt to be untrue. Yet if you realize what it means to say that nothing can be totally proved or disproved, then what you choose to have faith in is in fact what you choose to accept as true for the rest of your life.

What you have faith in is not simply what you believe to be true, but rather what you choose to believe is true because in your heart, mind, and soul, you want it to be true. You decide what you will have faith in, what you want to be true if anything at all is true. Having faith that something is true does not make it true, if it is not true, it is not true. Yet if what you have faith in is in fact true, it is true, period.

No matter how logical, rational, or scientific the arguments that are presented to you appear to be, we cannot prove that God exists or prove that God does not exist. We cannot prove that there is a life after death in a heaven or prove that a nihilistic death awaits us. Why then should you have faith God exists?

Again, if the message we conveyed to you about God was that he wants wars or sacrifices or other manner of destruction, then there would be no reason to have faith in him. But the message was and is that God who gave us love wants every human being to do that which is good. The message was and is that God wants every human being to love every other human being.

In our heart, mind, and soul we know and understand love. In our heart, mind, and soul we know and understand that it is "good" for each of us to love each other. If you have not completed your search of your heart, mind, and soul, if you do not yet understand that it is good to love each other, if you do not yet understand that we can and should do that which is good, then you will find it very difficult to find a reason to have faith in the existence of God. But if you have searched your heart, mind, soul, your very being, and know and understand love, you should want to, and choose to, have faith that a God exists who wants all people to do that which is good, a God who wants all people to love each other. If God does not exist then he does not exist, if God does exist then he does exist, period.

We believe that if God exists and gives each of us a non-physical life after death in a heaven filled with love, then our life both before and after physical death has meaning and value. We believe that if God exists, and in some manner beyond human comprehension grants existence to human beings even after the death of our bodies, then and only then life becomes more than a brief, isolated event. Then, and only then, life and love have meaning and purpose, and we can do that which is good.

Perhaps God has "revealed" to all or some of us that he exists. Yet even if God has not "revealed" this to you, he has given you the choice to have faith or not to have faith that he exists. Why should you have faith that God exists? Should we have faith that God exists because if God exists, God is good? We believe the answer to that question is that if we want good to exist and have meaning, if we want to do that which is good, we will choose to have faith that the Supreme Being, God, exists.

If love among people is good and meaningful and has purpose, it is good and meaningful and has purpose only if God exists and only because of God. If God makes it good for us to love each other in this life and in a world after death, and thus makes life worth living, then his existence alone gives us hope. It should be clear to all who want to do that which is good, who want to love, that they should have faith that God, the One who is good, exists.

It is God's will that we love each other, should we also love God? The answer to that question seems clear to us. We believe that without God, love would be destroyed by physical death and life would have no meaning or purpose. If our conclusions are right, without God there would be no reason for living. It is right to have faith in God and to love God, the One who is good. It is right to have faith in God and to love God, for without him love would be no more than one of many emotions that die with those who embrace them.

You should love God with the greatest love you can give. You should love God with all your heart, all your mind, all your soul, all your strength, for God alone makes it meaningful and right and good for us to love him and to love each other. You should love God with all your heart, all your mind, all your soul, all your strength, for God alone gives us hope that if we love him and love each other we will live forever in a joyous communion of love.

If you love God with all your heart, all your mind, all your soul, all your strength, you have chosen to do that which you can do, you can do no more, you should do no less. If you love God with all your heart, all your mind, all your soul, all your strength, you will do what God wants you to do, you will do God's will, you will love your neighbor as yourself.

Some two thousand years ago a man named Jesus said to all who would listen that God gave these commandments to all people, "You shall love the Lord your God with all your heart, and with all your soul, and with all your mind, and with all your strength." "You shall love your neighbor as yourself. There is no other commandment greater than these."

When asked who is my "neighbor" Jesus replied, "A man was on his way from Jerusalem down to Jericho when he fell into the hands of robbers, who stripped him, beat him, and went away leaving him half dead. It so happened that a priest was going down by the same road; but when he saw him, he went past on the other side. So too a Levite came to the place, and when he saw him he went past on the other side. But a Samaritan who was making the journey came upon him, and when he saw him he took pity on him. He went to him and bandaged his wounds, bathing them with oil and wine. Then he lifted him on his own animal, brought him to an inn, and took care of him there. The next day he took out two silver pieces and gave them to the innkeeper, and said, take care of him; and if you spend any more, I will repay you on my way back. Which of these three do you think was neighbor to the man who fell into the hands of the robbers?" The questioner answered, "the one who showed him kindness." Jesus said, "go and do likewise."

Who is your neighbor? With the possible exception of those who have totally rejected God, who if there is an eternal sin have committed the eternal sin (we briefly discuss the eternal sin in Distress & Depression in Appendix B, and in more detail in our other books), every person who loves you, every person who hates you, every enemy, every stranger, people of every continent, people of every race, every single human being in the entire world, everyone, is your neighbor. Jesus said that all who "keep the commandments" will live forever, continuing to exist after physical death in a state of never-ending joy.

Who was, or is, Jesus? Many people differ in who they believe Jesus to be. Many believe Jesus is the Son of God. There are many, many different beliefs as to what it means to say Jesus is God's son. Many believe Jesus was God incarnate. Other people believe Jesus was a prophet, given knowledge by God of the nature and meaning of life. Still others believe Jesus was not God but was a wise man with great insight into human existence.

Many people believe that Jesus and God are One, and that you must accept Jesus as God before you can know God and love God. We believe that even if you have not decided who you believe Jesus is, even if you do not believe that Jesus and God are One, you can and should love God with all your heart, with all your soul, with all your mind, with all your strength, and love your neighbor as yourself, and that out of that love you will choose to believe, and have faith in, what your heart, mind, and soul leads you to believe or have faith about Jesus.

Whoever you have faith or believe Jesus to be or have been, his message about life remains the same: "On these two commandments hang all the law and the prophets", "You shall love the Lord your God with all your heart, and with all your soul, and with all your mind, and with all your strength", "You shall love your neighbor as yourself", "There is no other commandment greater than these", "do this, and you will live." If we love as God would have us love we are doing the very best that we can do. There is nothing else that we can and should do. It is your choice to love as God would have you love, or not, period.

When you complete your search it will be clear to you what God means when he tells you that you can and should love the Lord your God with all your heart, with all your soul, with all your mind, with all your strength. When you complete your search you will also know and understand what God means when he tells you that you can and should love your neighbor "as yourself". You will know and understand that you can and should love your neighbor "as yourself", as if he or she was in your place, as if he or she was "you". You should give your neighbor the food that you would give yourself, the water that you would drink, the shelter that you would provide for yourself, the clothing that you would wear, etc.

You should do to your neighbor what you would have them do to you. You should give your neighbor the food, water, shelter, and clothing that you would have them give to you. You should care for them when they are sick as you would have them care for you if you were sick. You should visit them when they are in prison as you would have them visit you if you were in prison. You should give your neighbor real, true, pure, love. You should love your neighbor "as yourself".

What about traditional religious beliefs, theology and doctrine, baptism, sainthood, communion, all the beliefs and observances generations have cherished. What role do they play in our discussion of love?

If you understand love, the answer is clear that if you love God and your neighbor you will in every instance do the best you can to do what is right and good. That is all you can do.

Certainly loving God means you will help your neighbors when they are in need of help. Perhaps you will decide loving God requires you to make many changes in your religious beliefs, perhaps not. When you choose to love God and your neighbor, every choice you make will be made out of love. It is the choice to love God as he would have you love him, and out of that love to love people as he would have you love them, that is the one important choice, all other choices will be governed by that one profound decision. To love God and our neighbor as God would have us love is the complete answer to all our questions.

Even though many believe that God has already spoken to us, and that we have not listened, why does God not speak directly to each and every one of us and tell us that he exists? Perhaps God has not revealed to us that he exists in a manner that no one could question and has instead caused the observable physical universe to appear to follow deterministic laws, because he does not want us to know with absolute certainty that he does exist. Perhaps if we knew for an absolute fact that God exists, we would not choose to do God's will because we choose to love God and our neighbors, rather we would choose to do God's will to avoid loveless punishment. Perhaps God has not revealed to us that he exists so that we may have the freewill choice to have faith that God exists, and the freewill choice to love God and our neighbors, or not.

Why does God give us a choice to love or not to love? Why would God not create all of us in such a way that we must love as God would have us love? Perhaps the answer is that if evil did not exist, then not only would human beings not have a choice to do that which is bad, they would not have a choice to do that which is good. Perhaps if during our life on earth we did not have the freewill choice to do that which is good or do that which is bad, then we simply could not choose to love. Perhaps there is good and evil in this world so that we may choose love, and out of that love do that which is good.

We have completed a full circle back to the question, what is the meaning and purpose of life, yet it has become the question, should we believe God exists and have faith in him and love him? We have said that the reason we should have faith in and love God is because

65

if God exists, God is good, he gives meaning and purpose to life and love, and he wants us to love him and to love each other. A "why not" argument can be made that if God does not exist nihilists are probably right and death is the end, but since God might exist we should do what he would want us to do or we might end up tortured in some form of eternal loveless punishment. That logic sounds good, yet it leaves us with a feeling that those who love to avoid punishment don't really love at all. If we are to have faith in God, and love as he would have us love, we must choose to love him because we want to love as he would have us love, not because we want to avoid the consequences of not loving.

After you have searched your heart, mind, and soul and know and understand love, you must choose whether or not to believe that there is nothing in the world better than people loving other people. If you agree love is worth living for, and if love has meaning only if God exists, then you must choose whether or not to live for the one hope for human beings, that God exists. You should not have faith in God because you want to avoid a loveless, eternal punishment. You should have faith in God and love God because God is good. You should have faith in God and love God because you want to do that which is good, you want to love God and your neighbor.

What do I believe and have faith in? If we love as God would have us love, what do I have faith will happen to us after our physical death? I have absolute faith that if God exists God is good. I have absolute faith that if after physical death we exist in heaven or in a loveless eternal life, God gives us the freewill choice to do that which if we do we will live forever in heaven in the presence of God, the One who is good. Think about the real, true, pure, love you found when you searched your heart, mind, and soul, and you will know and understand what love in heaven would be like.

After one moment in heaven, we will know that every single moment of our existence, our entire being, will be filled with real, true, pure love, forever. All the illness, pain, and sorrow we experienced during our life on earth will vanish completely. In an instant, memories of even the worst that happened to us before our death will be overwhelmed by the love that surrounds us and will "disappear" forever. We will exist in the presence of real, true, pure, perfect love, forever. We will exist in the presence of God.

66

After many, many years of thought and discussion, I believe that there are many difficult questions which have answers that are unclear, uncertain, or unknown; that there are many thoughts and ideas that language cannot adequately express; that there is knowledge beyond human ability to know; that we cannot "prove" anything unless truth is revealed to us; etc. After completing my search of my heart, my mind, and my soul, I believe that we do not need to answer all the difficult questions, express in words all that we intuitively feel, know what we cannot know, "prove" what is beyond human ability to prove, etc.

I have faith that God exists and that it is God's will that I "love the Lord my God with all my heart, with all my soul, with all my mind, with all my strength" and "love my neighbor as myself". I have faith that if each moment of each day I love as God would have me love, when I die I will have done all I could do, all I should do, and I will live forever in a heaven filled with joyful love.

Love the Lord your God with all your heart, with all your soul, with all your mind, with all your strength.

Love your neighbor as yourself.

You will make your choice.

APPENDIX A - Fanatic Life or a Normal Life

What will our life be like if we love God and our neighbors as God would have us love? This is a very, very, difficult question. It is clear that if we love God and our neighbors we will give food to a starving child, water to a thirsty stranger, shelter to someone who is homeless and cold. This intuitive truth is strong and basic. Is it always good to give a drink of water to a thirsty neighbor? There may be situations where we must choose to give water to one of two neighbors based on which neighbor has a greater need for the water. There may be times when we are physically prevented from giving water to a thirsty neighbor, or when there may be other negative consequences of doing so. Yet it is clear that the basic, fundamental, statement "we should give water to a thirsty neighbor" is always true.

So where does all that we have said leave us? Does it leave us with pragmatic, situation ethics, where that which is "good" is determined by individual circumstances? It does not. Perhaps God will forgive us if we love God and our neighbor with a lesser love, yet that does not change the fact that you can and should "love the Lord your God with all your heart, with all your soul, with all your mind, with all your strength" and "love your neighbor as yourself", nothing more, nothing less, period.

If I love a neighbor who is hungry and thirsty what will I do? The answer is that I will give them food and water. No matter how hard I have tried to find another answer, if I love my neighbor and my neighbor is hungry and thirsty, I cannot imagine not giving them food and water. If you know and understand the love that God has given us, you know and understand that there is no other answer. This alone tells me that if we love our neighbor as God would have us love, we will not live a "normal life", we will live a "fanatic life".

So, what will we do if we live a "fanatic life"? If you love your neighbor as yourself, you will share God's word with them by word and deed so that each and every one knows and understands that they can and should choose to do that which is good, that they can and should choose to do God's will and live a joyous life forever in heaven. You will share your food with the hungry even if you are left with not enough to eat, give your only coat to someone who is cold, and find shelter for all the homeless people you meet.

Even though you may agree with what we have just said, you need to recognize that it is incredibly difficult to live a "fanatic life". It is relatively easy to accept that living a "normal life" filled with love for our family and friends is far better than living a life filled with selfish physical and emotional pleasure. It is not as easy to accept that a "normal life" is not the life that we should live, that it is not the "good life". It is extremely difficult to accept that we should live a life filled with "fanatic" and total acceptance of that which God would have us do.

This brings us to a very difficult question, if you "love the Lord your God with all your heart, with all your soul, with all your mind, with all your strength" and "love your neighbor as yourself", and you live in a world where some people do not choose to do God's will, will you ever do that which you would not do in a world where every person does God's will?

God has given each and every one of us the choice of giving food to our hungry neighbor or not. God has given each and every one of us the choice of doing physical harm to our neighbor or not. No matter what anyone else may choose to do, each of us has the choice to give food to a hungry neighbor or not, and each of us has the choice to do physical harm to a neighbor or not. I strongly believe that God would never have a neighbor choose not to give food to a hungry neighbor. I strongly believe that God would never have a neighbor choose to do physical harm to another neighbor. I simply do not believe that it is ever God's will that any of us choose not to give food to our hungry neighbor, or that any of us choose to do physical harm to our neighbor.

If your neighbor has plenty to eat yet is thirsty, and your neighbor refuses to share their food, it is not God's will that you say to your neighbor "share your food and then I will give water to you". It is God's will that you love your neighbor as yourself and give them a drink of water if they are thirsty. If your neighbor is doing physical harm to their neighbor, it is not God's will that you say to your neighbor "do not do physical harm to your neighbor and then I will not do physical harm to you". It is God's will that you love your neighbor as yourself and not do physical harm to them.

70

It is God's will that each and every moment of our lives each and every one of us do God's will, nothing less, nothing more, period. My hope is that if we live a "fanatic life", we will have done God's will on earth, and after our physical death we will live a joyous life in heaven, nothing could be better.

What if I am wrong about God wanting us to live a "fanatic life"? I understand that if I am wrong, the physical consequences of choosing to live a "fanatic life" may be horrendous. We live in a world where people choose to do evil. If we do not use minimal physical force to prevent physical harm, there will almost certainly be people who inflict excruciating pain and almost unimaginable tortures on our neighbors. If we do nothing to physically stop them, there will almost certainly be parents who savagely beat infants, mass murderers who kill innocent children, and brutal political leaders who commit genocide. If we do nothing to stop those who choose to do evil there will almost certainly be more wars, slavery, rape, and murder.

Most view life after death as a separate existence from life on earth, where those people who made physical life on earth as "good" as it can be will live a joyous life in heaven. The collective wisdom of generations of human beings who want to do that which is good is that God would have us live a "normal life". The vast majority of people, almost every person in the world, believes that we should do the best that we can to maximize the positive physical aspects of our lives on earth, while minimizing the negative. Perhaps the billions of people, including virtually every theologian and philosopher, who believe that we can and should love God and family and friends with a more complex love are right.

A "normal life" most would consider to be a "good life" is a life where each individual has strong spiritual beliefs and faith which they gladly share with other people. Such a normal life may include a strong family unit, a loving spouse and kids, and close relationships with relatives. The parents have jobs they enjoy that provide sufficient income for the family's comfort, and that give them plenty of time at home. Family members and extended family enjoy talking, playing games, helping with homework, working around the house, eating out, going to movies, etc. The adults and kids participate in sports and hobbies and take family vacations each year.

A "good" normal life includes volunteer work at hospitals, soup kitchens, homeless shelters, etc., and generous donations to charitable

71

organizations. The family accepts protection provided by police, military, and other government agencies using social programs, diplomacy, and the minimum force necessary to prevent one person from doing physical harm to another person. People who live such a "normal life" have a pleasant, happy, positive attitude toward all their "neighbors" including family, friends, and strangers. Almost every human being who wants to love God and their neighbor will choose to live a "normal life" that maximizes the positive physical aspects of their life on earth, without causing what they consider to be unacceptable negative consequences for themselves and their neighbors.

This is a "normal life" that most people would call a "good life". Indeed, almost everyone believes that this is the life that God would have us live. It is a life that focuses primary love and attention on family and self, and secondary love and attention on friends, while at the same time providing what each individual considers to be a generous amount of love, care, and help to those outside what is commonly known as their extended family.

Is this kind of "normal life" the life God would have us live, or not? I return to the question, if I love a neighbor who is hungry and thirsty what will I do? The answer is that I will give my neighbor food and water. My conclusion remains the same, I strongly believe that God would have us live a "fanatic life". Yet I may be wrong.

Even though I strongly believe that each and every one of us can and should live a "fanatic life", I intuitively believe that very, very, very, very, very few will choose to live such a life. Almost everyone, including theologians and philosophers, who chooses to love God and their neighbor will choose to love God and their neighbor with a "lesser love" than God would have them choose. Almost everyone who chooses to love God and their neighbor will choose to live what they consider to be a good "normal life".

God gave you the love that is in your heart, mind, and soul. God loves you. God forgives you not because of the good deeds you do, but because he loves you. I believe that God will forgive you if you love God and your neighbor, even with a lesser love.

If you, like almost every single human being in the world including me, are not willing to accept the physical consequences of living a "fanatic life", then live a "normal life" like the "normal life" we described. If you are unwilling to live a "fanatic life", love God with as much of your heart, your soul, your mind, and your strength as you are willing to love him with and love your neighbor as much as yourself as you are willing to love them, with the hope that God will forgive you.

Complete your search of your heart, mind, and soul, and know and understand the true, pure, real, love that God has given us. Complete your search of your heart, mind, and soul, and know and understand God's will, what God would have you do. You will decide what you will do. You will make your choice.

APPENDIX B - Distress & Depression

We have received comments from readers who tell us that our ideas caused them to be distressed or depressed. If you are one of those readers you need to consider the following. As human beings become anxious they often lose their focus and objectivity, and misinterpret what they are reading. If you understand what we are saying, there is absolutely no reason to be depressed by our ideas.

Why not? First, our conclusions may be right, we may have a permanent non-physical consciousness which gives meaning to life. Second, we may be wrong, life may have permanent existential meaning and value without a life after death. Third, if there is nothing after physical death you are free to live a life filled with both pain and joy, knowing that when you die the "pain" will be as if it never was.

No matter which of the three is right, depression and suicide may destroy the possibility of finding the meaning and purpose which may in fact exist in each and every human being's life, and the possibility of living a joyful life after physical death. We are a small part of the whole. Unless the answer is revealed to us by the whole, we can never know during our physical lives what really happens when our physical life ends. Life may have physical or non-physical meaning and value right now that we do not, and perhaps cannot during our physical lives, recognize and understand.

Beyond the fact that we cannot be sure we are right, nothing we have said changes the fact that all human beings can choose to do that which is good and live as positive a life as they can with the belief/faith that life may have meaning and purpose. This fact is extremely difficult to accept if you are searching for meaning in your life, you do not believe that there is a life after death, and you are discouraged or depressed before you start reading.

If your mind is not receptive and clear, when you read our ideas they may touch raw nerves and you may stop understanding what we are saying. If you do not agree that the possibility of "nothing" absolutely

75

eliminates suicide as an option then carefully reread our book, including "Afraid of Nothing", and this section until you understand why our conclusion is true.

There is no reason at all to reject the possibility that each of us has some kind of permanent physical or non-physical consciousness. There is no reason at all to reject the possibility that each of our lives may have meaning and purpose. There is no reason whatsoever not to search for an alternative to nihilism, to search for a reason for living, to seek meaning and purpose in our lives. We believe there is no reason not to search your heart, mind, and soul and choose to have faith, as we have faith, in a non-physical consciousness and life after physical death.

There is absolutely no reason whatsoever not to live for the possibility, however remote you may believe it to be, that you can make choices now that will lead you to a positive life that has meaning and value. It is very important to understand that every person can live a positive life for the rest of their lives, loving their neighbor, doing that which is good, with the hope that physical life does have existential meaning and purpose or that there is a life after death. There is no reason whatsoever to be depressed, there is every reason to do that which is good.

For help now, call 988 on your phone to reach the nationwide Suicide & Crisis Lifeline.

Eternal Sin

We have readers who indicate that they are distressed and depressed by the possibility that they may have committed the eternal sin. If God exists and if there is an eternal sin, then God gives us the choice to commit the eternal sin or not to commit the eternal sin. It would seem that those who have not committed the eternal sin would be distressed if they believed that they might have committed the eternal sin. It would seem that the very fact that someone is distressed by the belief that they may have committed the eternal sin may suggest that they have in fact not committed the eternal sin.

Physical and mental disorders cause extreme anxiety and depression and may lead a person to believe that they have committed the eternal sin when in fact they have not. If you are distressed and depressed by the possibility that you have committed the eternal sin, you need to talk with religious counselors. Talk to several people, especially mental health professionals if there is any possibility at all of psychological or emotional influences or problems, so that you may better determine what you have and have not done.

It can be very difficult to find qualified professionals, and even when you do find them, it can be very difficult to tell them about your fears. Find qualified professionals and talk to them. You need to overcome any reluctance you may have to talk with those who might help and be willing to allow them to help you decide what you really believe is true. Seek professional help now!

Call 988 on your phone to reach the nationwide Suicide & Crisis Lifeline.

Contact & Other Books

Our book, LOVE - In Search of a Reason for Living, is available in FREE eBook editions on our website LifeNotes.org and in the Apple and Google bookstores ($1 from Kindle).

It is also available in paperback from Amazon and other bookstores.

If you would like to help us maintain our publications please send a contribution to:

LifeNotes, Inc., 838 E High St Box 130, Lexington, Ky 40502 Email: Comments@ws5.com

V 11-11-11-12-12-22-2-25-U

www.ingramcontent.com/pod-product-compliance
Lightning Source LLC
Chambersburg PA
CBHW070550030426
42337CB00016B/2425